Forecasting Revenu For Small E

M000274176

Using Statistical Analytics

ELEANOR WINSLOW

Published by Auditmetrics
Copyright © 2020 Auditmetrics
Boston, Massachusetts
ISBN- 978-0-578-79725-0

Inquiries about free AI Assisted Account Sampling Software

info@auditmetrics.com

Table of Contents

Introduction

Forecasting business revenue and expenses is as much art as science. Many business managers complain that building forecasts with any degree of accuracy takes a lot of time. It is better spent selling rather than planning. But few financial institutions will put money in a business if it's unable to provide a set of thoughtful forecasts. More important, proper financial forecasts will help develop operational and staffing plans that will create a more efficient business environment. Ongoing internal audits and forecasting trends using regular random sampling is key in measuring the pulse of business activity..

> *Market analysis and operations research discussions can involve very complex procedures that may be beyond the reach of small business managers. With this book and software the complexity of properly sampling, conducting statistical analysis and documenting accounts is handled by Auditmetrics AI assisted software that is made available with the book. It prepares the business manager to conduct sophisticated analysis that is inexpensive and easy to use. The AI assistance starts with the manager to first decide on a margin of error and the software then guides the process through to the finish.*

Separate statistical software is not necessary. Excel offers a wide range of statistical functions which can be used to calculate a single value or an array of values in the Excel worksheet. The Excel Analysis Toolpak is an add-in that provides the statistical analytic tools that is used in this book. Microsoft Excel Professional and the Windows operating system are the only requirements.

It has been our experience that most accountants and individuals that self-administer their business are generally well versed in Excel. Appendices are included to cover the basics of using MS Excel in selecting a stratified random sample and how to convert QuickBooks standard reports into an Excel data matrix that can be read in by Auditmetrics AI.

The book is divided into two main sections:

PART I – The Statistical Method - In this section is covered the statistical principles of analyzing empirically derived account data that is the underpinning of economic analysis. Two fundamental ideas are uncertainty and variation. Data is used to help explore and understand the dynamics of the business environment. What leads to that uncertainty is data variation that is inherent in financial data. In this section is covered the basic measurement of central tendency, variation and uncertainty such as the mean, standard deviation and probability. It is presented at a basic level for those who have minimal experience in statistics. For those who have taken courses in statistics, this will be a refresher that focuses on statistical methods used in economic analysis and market research.

Part II – Forecasting Revenue and Expenses Using Regression –
In this Section is a discussion of using one of the most powerful tools in forecasting future economic activity. It begins by covering the core principles of regression, starting with bivariate modeling and progressing to multiple and non-linear regression. The building and interpreting of regression output is accomplished by using MS Excel built-in functions. Though Excel can do all the regression calculations and outputs covered in this section, it is still important to review the underlying mechanics that is provided in Part I.

Auditmetrics V6 Software

Version 5 data access architecture was based on a direct read of MS Excel spreadsheets and MS Access relational databases. Though this design is user friendly, over time it proved to be problematic. As we expanded our reach to larger data sets, version 5 proved to be untenable.

With large data sets the V5 original architecture turned out to have technical and practical limitations. Excel spreadsheet size limitation is a million records. So as we needed to access accounts with several million records, Excel as a direct data read became untenable.

Another problem is upgrades of MS Office and Windows do come with issues. Going from an older version to an upgrade means, at best, minor changes in new software coding but at times whole segments of code eventually becoming outdated. We therefore decided to get back to basics and use a standardized international data structure that is not controlled by any proprietary business interest. All major accounting, database and statistical software can generate that same common universal data structure, text files. Text files are the most efficient data source for input-output (IO) functions. Because of that conversion, auditmetrics V6 can process 5 million records in a matter of seconds on a laptop greatly outperforming V5. Text files are sometimes called ASCII files which stands for American Standard Code for Information Interchange. The Internet Assigned Numbers Authority (IANA) prefers the updated name US-ASCII. This file structure is universally available and is universally transferable to and from all major database and statistical software including Microsoft Excel.

What is practical for the small business manager?

A good starting point is look at what is readily available. Almost all business use fairly sophisticated computerized accounting systems. They all have the ability to generate reports that summarize customer activity as it relates to the bottom line. Those reports can also be used to generate data for more sophisticated analysis. See Appendix II on how that can be accomplished. Most systems also allow a dump of account data into an Excel file, text data files such as comma separated variable (.csv) or tab delimited text files (.txt) that can be readily read into the auditmetrics software. The .csv is a special text file that can be read in directly by Excel.

If not sure how to proceed, seek the help of your accounting system vendor. It should be standard for any quality vendor to be able to meet all of your data needs.

Part I – Basic Statistical Principles

Statistics is about solving practical problems by collecting and using information derived from data. The aim of this section is to study in more detail statistical methods for analyzing data primarily as they relate to the statistical audit and forecasting. There are three main goals for statistical analysis:

Goal I – Descriptive Statistics is to display and make sense of data using common measures and displays and how it can be organized in databases.

Goal II – Inferential Statistics is to generalize from a sample to a total population that could not be examined in its entirety. The issue of probability is discussed.

Goal III – Model Building - is to develop a model of real world processes. Statistical theory is used to develop a probabilistic model that best describes the relationship between dependent and independent variables. This is a discussion that will provide the business analyst with an expanded set of very useful and powerful statistical methods.

I.   Descriptive Statistics

Descriptive statistics are used to describe, present, summarize, and organize data, either through numerical calculations or graphs or tables. Some of the common descriptive measurements in statistics involve dataset measures involving central tendency and variability. Descriptive statistical analysis is used to get a quick and systematic view of data and is a very important part of understanding the data needed for forecasting. Descriptive statistical analysis of the dataset is absolutely crucial. Many individuals often skip this step and therefore lose insight about the data, which can lead to an improper business plan.

A good descriptive statistic is a summary that describes important quantitative features of a collection of data usually from a sample. Descriptive statistics is distinguished from inferential statistics by its aim to summarize and understand sample data, rather than use that data to make decision about the population from which the sample was derived. This generally means that descriptive statistics, unlike inferential statistics, is not selected on the basis of probability theory. Even when sample data is used to make inferences, descriptive statistics are generally also used to provide necessary background information.

Data – Information Building Blocks

This book relies heavily on accounting data but it is up to business analysts to include additional data that goes beyond dollars and the bottom line. The simplest way to start is to merge account information with secondary qualitative and quantitative data. For example a simple brief questionnaire asking customers rating their service, suggestions for improvement and new options etc. This data can be merged with the straight accounting data of dollar and cents.

Larger scale data sources via census and other publicly available data can also be a valuable source of customer demographic input. Customer demographics is valuable so that business plans can be tailored for specific market segments. A message targeting senior citizens will be different than that for a teenager. The challenge is how to link secondary add-on marketing data with account information.

Having an understanding of database design is very valuable. A relational database is an easily understandable design that is the basis of Microsoft Access. It can be used to creates tables each derived from separate independent files. The relational database management system (RDMS) creates a mechanism that links those individual files into an integrated unified system. It allows one to easily find specific information. It also allows one to sort based on any field and generate reports that contain selected fields from each table. The fields and records are represented as columns (fields) and rows (records) in a table.

With a relational database, you can quickly compare information because of the arrangement of data in columns. The relational database model takes advantage of this uniformity to build completely new tables out of information from existing tables. In other words, it uses the relationship of similar data to increase the speed and versatility of the database.

The "relational" part of the name comes into play because of key field relationships. Each table contains a column or columns that other tables can key onto to gather information. This architecture can create a single smaller targeted table for specific analysis. The following exhibit is an example of how revenue information can be linked to customer data.

Customer Table:

FirstName	LastName	Street	City_Town	Zip	Phone	Account ID
John	Smith	21 Maple	Holly	99999	555-148-3287	100001
Sarah	Brown	3 Oak	Hamlet	99998	555- 396-1899	100002
Judy	Taylor	267 Elm	Mid Town	99997	555 470 8143	100003

Account Table:

Transaction ID	Sales	Department	Date	etc.	etc.	Account ID
2	216.76	1001	Jan. 10			100001
4	255.02	1001	Jan. 12			100001
5	299.24	1001	Jan. 13			100003
8	405.79	1002	Jan. 15			100002
11	562.08	1002	Jan. 20			100002
15	105.06	1001	Feb. 1			100003
17	201.99	1002	Feb. 6			100003

The relationship described above is one to many. For each customer there can be several transactions. The ingredients are available to do a projection of sales by zip code. This will help in determining local market characteristics. If the account table also has demographics data, such as age and gender, then there can also be an analysis of specific market demographic segments. These factors are essential ingredients in performing market research.

How to use MS Access

MS Access is a powerful relational database that is easy to use. Below is a brief summary of how to get started in setting up a database. If you can put your relevant account data on an Excel file, Access can use it to load it on to a table. Below is a brief overview in setting up an Access database. IT is beyond the scope of this book to go into great detail but there are an ample number of web sites that can also enhance knowledge.

MS Access is a powerful tool in creating and implementing a RDMS without the need to use code. It can be done by use of wizards or using the following steps.

- Determine the Aim of Your Relational Database.
- Define tables, fields and primary key index.
- Determine the relationships between tables.

1. **Build a Microsoft Access database**

- Start Microsoft Access, and then create a new blank database named
  e.g."MyAccess.mdb".
- Create a new table named e.g. "Sales Account" by following these steps:
  -Under Objects, click Tables.

  -Double-click Create table by using wizard.

  -Verify that a new table named "Sales Account" has been created.

2. **Create database relationships in access**

- Create a relationship - Create a relationship in an Access desktop database
- On the Database Tools tab, in the Relationships group, click Relationships.
- If you haven't yet defined any relationships, the Show Table dialog box automatically appears.
- Select one or more tables, and then click Add. After you have finished adding tables, click Close.

Data Field Types

> Qualitative Scale
> > Nominal
> > Ordinal
> Quantitative Scale
> > Interval
> > Ratio

Nominal Scale

A nominal level of measurement deals strictly with qualitative Data. Observations are simply assigned to predetermined categories.

Examples: account type; gender; class membership i.e. ; race, socio-demographic, Color of eyes.

Key Characteristics: Can't perform mathematical operations on the categories. No meaningful ranking of the categories.

However, one can count the number within each category that can be manipulated mathematically.

Ordinal Scale

Ordinal Level of Measurement: has all the properties of nominal data with the added feature that we can rank-order the values from highest to lowest.

Examples: Ranking individual students based on class rank, rank accounts based on total dollar volume, also ranking of categories e.g. high, middle, low income individuals.

Key Characteristics: Can't perform mathematical operations on the categories, but the categories or individuals can be ranked in order.

It can be considered at times quantitative or qualitative, are you ranking the individual or category?

Interval Scale

The interval level of measurement allows for quantitative comparisons among data, but with some restrictions. The lack of a true zero value prevents the use of multiplication and division in the comparisons.

Classic Examples: Temperature in degrees C and F; IQ scores

Key Characteristics: Quantitative data only. Differences between values can be measured but multiplication and division yield no useful information because a true zero value does not exist. For example temperature scales or only arbitrary ranges between the boiling and freezing point of water where zero has no quantitative meaning, it is just another point of the scale.

Effect of true zero point:

For example, you can't say that 20 degrees C is half as warm as 40 degrees C.

If you were to say that 20F is half as warm as 40F, and then say that 20C is half as warm as 40C, would the amount of difference in heat energy be equal in both cases? NO!

However, the Kelvin scale does have a true zero value. At 0 degrees K (absolute zero −273.15°C) there is no heat, kinetic energy. This is not true for 0 degrees C or 0 degrees F. You can say 400 degrees K has twice the heat or kinetic energy of 200 degrees K.

Ratio Scale

Ratio Level of Measurement: "Ratio data has all the features of interval data with the added benefit of a true 0 point. The term "true zero point" means that a 0 data value indicates the absence of the object being measured."

Example: In the statistical audit it is the dollar value.

$20 is half the value of $40

Broadest range of statistical tests available to you when you have ratio data – accurate measurement essential

Moving from one Scale to Another

Ratio /Interval -> Ordinal -> Nominal

Example: Net Income Book-> Net Income Ranking -> No. Profit/No. Loss

It is always possible to go from Ratio/Interval scale to Ordinal Then to Nominal Scale:

- Qualitative
    - Nominal Scale
    - Ordinal Scale
- Quantitative
    - Interval Scale
    - Ratio Scale

Example: *Start with account receivables for each customer. The dollar values represent the ratio scale of measurement. That means you not only know the interval between each data point but there is a true zero point. Customer #1 has an AR of $2,200 and customer #2 an AR at $1,200 then the interval between the two is $1,000. If the total book is $10,000 we can also state that customer #1 represents $2,200/$10,000 or 22% of all account receivable. This gives us the most complete information about the book and customers.*

Suppose we want to target the top 20 customers in terms of accounts receivables without releasing actual dollars. It is an easy matter to rank the customers such as customer #1 is number one, customer #2 is number 2 two etc. There are several statistical methods that can be used to handle ordinal level of data. However some information is lost in translating from ration/interval to ordinal . The interval between customer #1 and customer #2 is unknown.

The same data can be converted to the nominal scale of measurement sometimes called categorical data. Suppose we want to deal with just two groups, those who have outstanding balance and those who do not. These two groups require different handling so such a dichotomy make administrative sense. Administratively there is a collection of individuals who require action.

Making Sense of Assembled Data

Descriptive statistics are summaries of data that is collected to explain patterns and key specific monitoring measurements of the data. Many accounts generate large numbers of data points, and to make sense of all that data, analysts use summary statistics and other methods to explain the pattern in the data. This provides a better understanding of overall tendencies within the distribution of the data and is also an important first step toward the implementation of inferential statistics.

Even if the primary aim of an analysis involves inferential statistics, descriptive statistics are still used to give a general summary and a basis for statistical decision making. Describing the population using tools such as frequency distribution, percentages, and other measures of central tendency like the mean are the fundamental tools of descriptive statistics. When using a specific statistical inference test (e.g. confidence intervals), descriptive statistics can help in summarizing data in simple quantitative measures.

The descriptive statistics for account data discussed so far was primarily to describe a single variable, dollars (univariate analysis). There are times when more than one variable (bivariate/multivariate analysis) should be used to better understand accounts. In the case of more than one variable, descriptive statistics can help summarize relationships between different variables using tools such as scatter

15

plots. Multivariate methods are useful in building a model of the world which is a more complex form of inferential statistics.

Descriptive Statistics Summarization Types

Account analysis can generate large numbers of data points, and to make sense of that data, analysts use statistics and other methods that summarize the data, providing a better understanding of overall tendencies of account data. There are two major types of descriptive methods that can be performed in Excel:

- Sorting/grouping tables and illustration/visual displays

- Summary statistics i.e. mean, standard deviation etc.

- Excel's "=Frequency" function

- Excel's Pivot Table

Details of how to use these tools will be discussed in more detail in the section about forecasting using regression analysis.

Summary Statistics not only help in making sense of data but some key summary statistics are critical in the development of inferential statistics methods. There are two types of summary statistics in statistical inference:

- Measures of central tendency
- Measures of dispersion

Measures of central tendency capture general trends within the data and are calculated and can be expressed as the mean, median, and mode. A mean tells auditors the mathematical average of all of a data set:

Mean is the 'average' or total dollar value divided by the number of data points. It has a number of useful statistical properties such as its use in inferential statistics. However, it can be sensitive to extreme scores, sometime referred to as outliers.

The arithmetic mean of a dataset is more formally defined as being equal to the sum of the numerical values of each and every observation divided by the total number of observations. Symbolically, if we have a data set consisting of the values X_1, X_2, ., X_n

then the arithmetic mean represented by the Greek letter mu is defined by the formula:

$$\mu = \Sigma X_i / N$$

Where:

μ is the mean of the account dollar value

N is the total number of dollar transactions in the audit population.

X_i is dollar value for ith observation which can vary from 1 to N

The mean as a measure of average of the dataset does have limitations. There are other measures of central tendency that may be preferable to the mean. For example, most income summary statistics usually use the median as a fair representation of the distribution of income and other financial data. Why? The mean is affected by extreme values. This in turn can give a false impression of "average income". For example, if you obtain a sample of incomes of middle class individuals that should reflect national statistics. But if for some reason a billionaire is somehow included in the sample, the mean would be weighted by that extreme value, therefore resulting in an average that would be weighted at a very high value.

The median is another measure of central tendency. The median is the value separating the higher half count of a data sample, a population, or a probability distribution, from the lower half. In simple terms, it may be thought of as the "middle" value of a data set. For example, in the data set {1, 3, 3, 6, 7, 8, 9}, the median is 6, the fourth number in the sample. It cuts the number of observations into the upper half or 50% and lower half. This is also referred to as the 50th percentile.

Below is a review of the total dollar value of client contracts signed by a consulting firm. The mean would be the total dollar value of the contracts which is $3,410,000 divided by 25 contracts which equals $136,400. If management wants to impress investors then it could claim its average contract dollar value is $136,400. It would be true and good spin, but is it a true reflection of average contract value? The 156k cutoff is weighted by one very large contract. With the median, which is 40k, half of the contracts are above and half below this value. This provides a clearer view of the typical contact value, especially if the 2.25 million dollar contract is a rare event.

Contract Value (x1000)	Number Contracts	Central Tendency Measures
$2,250	1	
$156	1	Mean 136k is weighted average
$102	2	
$64	1	
$52	3	
$45	4	
$40	1	Median 40k, 12 above 12 below
$30	12	Mode 30k, most frequent
Total	25	

Another measure of central tendency is the mode. The mode of a set of data values that appears most often. It is the value that is most likely to be sampled and in this instance the typical contract size that is managed by the firms employees.

The measures of central tendency provides a concise measure that can be used as a single value to describe a set of data by identifying the central position of that data. But as we found out in our discussion of a firm's contract size, the spread of the data is also an important consideration. How useful would be contract mean in summarizing future contract sizes? Not very good because it is heavily weighted by one extreme value.

Properties of mean:

- The 'average' score—total score divided by the number of scores
- Has a number of useful statistical properties, especially for inferential methods.
- Many statistics are based on mean when testing hypothesis
- Sensitive to 'outliers', extreme cases that just happened to end up in your sample by chance

Other measures give us an idea what the 'typical' value in a distribution:

- Mode: the most frequent score in a distribution
- Median: the midpoint or mid-score in a distribution.
  - (50% observations above/50% observations below)
  - Insensitive to extreme scores.

Besides the mean's use in statistical inference, a measure of spread is also of considerable importance. A measure of central tendency can be used as a prediction of future outcomes, but it is the spread of the data that will influence the prediction's precision.

Measures of Dispersion purpose

- Look at how widely scattered are the scores
- Several groups with identical means can be more or less diverse
- A standard measure on how data is distributed is measured by how far or close individual observations are from the mean

Range as a measure of dispersion

- Distance between the highest and lowest scores in a distribution;
- sensitive to extreme scores;
- compensate by calculating interquartile range (distance between the 25th and 75th percentile points) which represents the range of scores for the middle 50% of a distribution
- Usually used in combination with other measures of dispersion

Standard Deviation and Variance:

- There are two related measures of dispersion that are valuable in determining the spread of the data. It is the spread of data that determines the uncertainty of using the mean in projecting future outcomes.
- Usually designated by the Greek letter sigma

Let's start with a simple set of data: 0, 25, 50, 75, 100 to examine the interplay of standard deviation and variance.

The mean is:

$$\mu = \Sigma X_i / N = \$250$$

Let's examine the deviations $(X - \mu)$ from the mean and square those deviations:

21

X	X-μ	$(X-\mu)^2$
$0	-$50	$2,500
$25	-$25	$625
$50	$0	$0
$75	$25	$625
$100	$50	$2,500
$\Sigma=$	$0	$6,250

The mean is a weighted average so all deviations above the mean cancels out those below the mean. The measure of spread around the mean is a two stage process. Each deviation is squared which eliminates the net zero effect of summing deviations above and below the mean. The units are a scale of square units but to get back to the original scale is to take the square root of the square deviations.

Step 1 Measure Variance:

Variance is an average of squared deviations:

$$\sigma^2 = \Sigma(X_i - \mu)^2/N$$
$$= \$6,250 / 5 = \$1,250$$

Variance is in itself is an important measure useful in statistical inference. For example, there is a statistical analytical method called analysis of variance (ANOVA). It has uses in testing differences among the means of several random samples or the efficiency of the regression mathematical model. These are two important analytical methods that will be discussed later.

Step 3 Measure Standard Deviation:

Squared units must eventually be reduced to the original scale by taking the square root of variance. This helps in getting a sense of the spread of the data and can also be used in calculating the coefficient of variation (COV=σ / μ) which is a standardized measure of dispersion of a frequency distribution. A COV can be run for any given quantifiable data, and otherwise unrelated COVs can be compared to one another in ways that other measures cannot.

Standard Deviation:

$$\sqrt{\sigma^2 = \sum_{i-1}^{N}(X_i - \mu)^2/N}$$

$$= \sqrt{\$1,250} \quad = \$35.4$$

Auditmetrics® Descriptive Statistics

Reminder! free software contact info@auditmetrics.com

The software as part of this book is the "Small Business V6" learning version that has some file size limitations. It is not ideal for use in data mining techniques that involves processing high volume datasets. It is is better served by "Professional V6". It can handle accounts with millions of records and includes forensic accounting techniques using Benford formula. The software was originally developed for the Massachusetts Department of Revenue, Audit bureau, in conducting sales and use taxes audits. For Professional 6:

Search for "Auditmetrics AI" at Microsoft Store

The same sampling for forecasting revenue and expenses.

If you have obtained the Auditmetrics software that complements this book, there will be a standard list of descriptive statistics of sampled accounts. In the software's initial screen after calculating of the suggested detail cutoff a useful list of descriptive statistics are also displayed:

23

- Suggested Detail Cutoff
- Interquartile Range
- Proportion Dollar Volume Less $100
- Audit Population:
  - Mean (μ),
  - Standard Deviation (σ)
  - Total Frequency (N)
- Sample:
  - Mean ($\overline{X}$),
  - Standard Deviation (s)
  - Total Frequency (n)

In using account samples enhancing statistical efficiency involves using a detail cutoff. This is a standard feature of statistical audits. This is the cutoff above which 100% of the transactions are reviewed. eliminating the largest transactions from sampling, reduces the variability (standard deviation) of the remaining transactions from which a sample is drawn. This enhances statistical efficiency. There are rules of thumb to determine what size of transaction should be the cutoff. For example, one rule of thumb is to select all large transactions that account for 25% to 35% of the total book value of all transactions. The detail stratum isolates those high dollar transactions that have the greatest economic impact. This also helps provide for a more stable mean of the remaining transactions to be sampled since it is a measure greatly impacted by large values.

The detail cutoff is calculated by the Auditmetrics algorithm that uses percentile ranks of different dollar cutoffs. A percentile (or a centile) is a measure used in statistics indicating the value below which a given percentage of observations in a group of observations falls. For example, the 20th percentile is the value (or score) below which 20% of the observations and 80% above that value.

The interquartile range represents the dollar range between the 25th and 75th percentile ranks. The interquartile range (IQR) is a number

24

that indicates how spread out scores are and tells us the range of the middle of a set of scores. The primary advantage of using the interquartile range rather than the range (largest value – lowest value) for measuring spread is that the interquartile range is not sensitive to outliers.

In finance there is a special percentile called Value at Risk. It is a standard measure to assess the quantity under which the value of the portfolio is not expected to sink within a given period of time and given a confidence value. It estimates the probability of how much investments might lose in a set time period. It is used by firms and regulators in the financial industry to gauge the amount of assets needed to cover possible losses. The probability is derived from percentile ranks of the normal curve. It is a concept that business can use for its revenue targets.

Another descriptive measure displayed on the initial screen is the percentage of values below $100. There are times when conducting an audit there may be certain values below which it is not economic in terms of labor costs and other costs to include for review. This is especially important in conducting internal audits.

> **Example:** *For most expense and sales audits, the business manager is looking for two things: sales transactions that were not properly managed leading to a reduction in revenue and those expenses that were not properly handled. For example a medical office audit may find that a certain percentage of claims submitted to an insurance company were not properly filled out leading to revenue loss. Chasing low dollar transactions may not be worth the staff time labor costs.*

The final list of descriptive statistics are the mean and standard deviation of both the audit population and the derived sample. Notice that descriptive statistics for the population is designated by Greek letters and for the sample English letters.

I.   Inferential Statistics

This section covers a basic overview of statistical inference as it relates to the sampling of accounts. The Auditmetrics AI software guides the business financial manager through the process of obtaining random sampling from business accounts. In addition statistical inference properties are documented using Excel files. Auditmetrics.com also offers PowerPoint slides for those who want to dig deeper into statistical theory.

Contact us at: info@auditmetrics.com .

Statistical account sampling can involve using several statistical tests. We frequently want to know if two or more accounts differ from one another with respect to some parameter they share such as sales, accounts receivable, account payable etc.. These comparisons generally involve using sample statistics to estimate the value of an account parameter. In the confidence interval test, these estimates are compared using a statistical test to identify a difference or lack thereof. The basic test is if the sample confidence interval actually includes the audit population parameter. one can conclude the sample is an unbiased representation of the audit population. This is a common type of statistical test.

The Nature of Random Samples

Below exhibit outlines the nature of the random sample process:

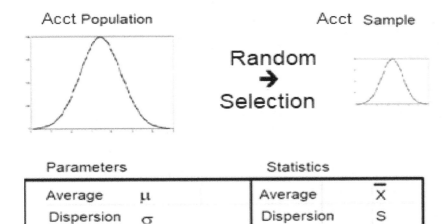

- **A parameter is a number that describes the population**. It is a fixed number, but in practice we generally do not know its value. In Computerized business accounts if our parameter of interest is the mean, it can be determined by the business accounting standard reports. Auditmetrics software uses this fact to determine the validity of a sample statistic.

- **A statistic is a function of the sample**, i.e., it is a quantity whose value can be calculated from sample data. It is a random variable with a specific distribution function, i.e. the normal curve. Sample statistics are used to make inferences about population parameters.

- **Random sample variables:** $X1, $X2,…,$Xn account data are said to form a random sample of size n. if the $Xi's are independent random variables then each follows the normal distribution. That is each $Xi has the same probability of being selected.

Sampling in Business

Sampling is a technique of selecting a subset of the account population in using statistical inference methods to estimate characteristics of the whole population. Auditmetrics using AI assistance automatically provides sample estimates of population parameters. Random sampling is a cost-effective method in drawing conclusions about population parameters.

For example, if a business would like to research the market demand for a new product, it is almost impossible to conduct a research study that involves everyone. In this case, the market researcher will use a sample of people from different demographics to provide feedback on rating the new product.

Types of sampling:

Probability sampling: technique where a researcher sets a selection of a few criteria and chooses members of a population randomly. It is a sampling technique in which researchers choose samples from a larger population using the theory of probability. This sampling method considers every member of the population for selection and forms samples based on a fixed process.

Convenience non-probability sampling: the business researcher chooses individuals for research on the basis of what elements are easy to obtain. . This sampling method is not a fixed or predefined selection process. This makes it difficult for all elements of a population to have equal opportunities to be included in a sample. For example A business manager asks customers before they leave to rate their service for a week or two. This may provide valuable insights as to potential opportunities or problems. As indicated by their name, convenience samples are definitely easy to obtain. There is virtually no difficulty in selecting members of the population for a convenience sample. But, there is a price to pay for this lack of effort: convenience samples are virtually worthless in statistical theory.

The reason a convenience sample cannot be used for statistical analytics is that we are not assured that it is representative of the population that it was selected from. For example all of the customers for the last week may share some common characteristics, it cannot be assured that they represent all of the customers of record. So such sampling can be biased.

There are two types of probability sampling techniques relevant in sampling business accounts:

- **Simple random sampling:** This is one of the easiest probability sampling techniques that helps in saving time and resources. It is a reliable method of obtaining information where every single member of a population is chosen randomly, merely by chance. Each individual has the same probability of being chosen to be a part of a sample.

  Example: *if a company has a list of 5000 customers, in a random sample each customer would have a 1/5000 chance of being selected.*

Stratified random sampling: is a method in which the researcher divides the population into smaller groups that don't overlap. They are organized to draw a random sample from each group separately. It is he inherent sampling technique used by Auditmetrics. This topic is discussed in great detail in the book: "Statistical Audit Automation"*

Both Kindle and paperback versions are available on Amazon

    Example: *a researcher looking to analyze an account of total sales by customer. Sales income will be divided into strata (groups) according to total sales value: less than $2,000, $2,100– $3,000, $3,100 to $4,000, $4,000 to $5,000, etc. By doing this, the researcher can observe the characteristics of people belonging to different income groups. Business marketers can analyze which income groups to target and which ones to eliminate to create a roadmap that would bear fruitful results.*

Benefits of probability sampling

There are multiple uses of probability sampling:

- **Reduce Sample Bias:** Using the probability sampling method, the bias in the sample derived from a population is minimized.

- **Create an Accurate Sample:** Probability sampling helps the market researchers plan and create an accurate as well as an unbiased sample.

Sampling and Data Types

Attribute vs. Variable Sampling

There are two basic types of data sampling techniques: either variable sampling or attribute sampling. When data is measured on a quantitative scale, it is variable data e.g. weight, length, and in sampling accounts, dollars. Variable sampling is standard for sales and use tax audits or in any auditing situation where one wants to measure specific dollar quantities, such as total dollars in error or in compliance with regulations or other standards. The Internal Revenue Service (IRS) has established statistical guidelines that are becoming a national standard. Variable stratified sampling techniques are mathematical formula driven. The fundamental goal of variable sampling is to answer the question of quantity or "how much?"

Attribute sampling data are classified categorically (nominal scale). For example, data tracking whether accounts receivable items are past due, they could be categorized as "yes" or "no." Attribute sampling is integral to opinion polling and market research where the pollster seeks the characteristics of targeted subsets of the population. In those environments, data stratifications are situation dependent. For example a pollster or market researcher may be interested in demographic breakdowns of potential customers such as socioeconomic status and gender. There are multiple variations of attributes but to the business financial planner, they should ultimately relate to that all-important variable, dollars.

Attribute sampling is classification dependent. For example, an accountant may want to examine customer base in terms of sex, age category or other sociodemographic classification. These are attributes that are mutually exclusive, and the purpose of the audit would be to answer the question "how many?" are there in each category. There are several types of attribute questions that may be very useful for analytic purposes.

Examples of typical attribute sampling breakdowns are:

- 20 of 100 accounts receivable invoices were past due

- 10 of 40 inventory invoices greater than $1,000 contained a signature

- 19 of 20 fixed assets purchases had a supporting authorization document

- 2 of 11 supplier invoices indicated the early payment discount was not taken

- 13 of 211 journal entries were posted to the wrong account

The results of an attribute sampling test, such as those above, are then compared to a criterion previously established. If the test results are worse than the standard, then the test has failed and accounts should be carefully examined for possible remedies. For example, if the acceptable proportion of past due accounts receivable invoices is 3% and the sample estimated rate is 20%, it will be necessary to impose additional controls, retrain staff, and/or alter invoice management procedures to reduce the number of past due invoices.

There are times when an accountant can exploit the benefits of both methods of sampling. The auditor may be interested in revenue and cost estimates (variables) by different segments (attributes) of the business or class of transaction. As mentioned previously, variable sampling procedures are easier to design and implement because the methodology is largely formula driven.

The quantitative nature of dollars provides more information about each unit of observation and therefore, in statistical terms, a more powerful estimate. An attribute sample is a collection of individual observations based on a common classification. Therefore, each data point is part of a collection, each indistinguishable therefore lacking a certain amount of specificity rendering projections with less statistical power.

The Hybrid Approach and the Learning Experience

The Auditmetrics AI (available at Microsoft Store) system provides a step by step sample methodology that combines the characteristics of both variable and attribute sampling techniques. This combined approach is the methodology many auditors use. In those audits, the auditor is interested in "how many" transactions in an account are in error, such as having a revenue not properly charged. But the auditor is also interested in "how many" transactions are in error, but also what is the dollar volume in revenue lost?". If the attribute data is customer centric, then the basic question is for example not only how many men and women are customers but also how much is the dollar impact of each attribute.

A well-chosen representative random sample can be used to project total dollar amounts that can be broken into any attribute(s) of interest. Variable data allows the business analyst to minimize the amount of statistical error when performing financial projections. First step is to set up a variable sampling technique to obtain a representative random sample of an account based on dollar value. Once the dollar based random sample is drawn, then one can go through the analytic steps to determine the validity of the sample which can be completed using Auditmetrics AI assisted software.

Because accounts are commonly processed in almost all businesses electronically through standard software such as QuickBooks® various key economic characteristics of the total book of transactions is known, usually through standard computerized reports. It is possible to statistically test whether a sample drawn is a valid statistical subset and not an outlier. For example if sample measures, such as total book value, vary greatly from known book value derived from accounting software, then the sample validity criteria can be called into question. If that particular sample is termed a "statistical outlier" then a new sample should be drawn. There are a myriad of variables that can be tested in this manner including revenue, expenses, tax credits etc.

*Though our goal is to forecast revenue and expenses, the Auditmetrics system makes it very easy to do an internal audit at the same time. Ideally this should be a first step. It does not make sense to project future outcomes based on data that may have many errors leading to invalid projections. **A valid sample is a necessary requirement for projecting expenses and revenue.***

Below are examples of issues relevant to statistical sampling of accounts:

What is the error rate of paid medical insurance claims. i.e. Due to plan coverage and eligibility requirements benefits are not valid but were paid.	The analyst wants to know not only how many claims have been improperly paid but also the percentage of dollar volume in error.
The data in the journal. What is the amount of deductions not supported by Non-Taxable Transaction Certificates?	The auditor needs to know percent of and specific dollar amount.
Do sales summary reports match up with credit card company reports?	The auditor wants to know if income statement entries match credit card receipts.

How often are invoices voided without explanation?	Here, the analyst wants to know a specific number of invoice errors but also its dollar impact.
Do managers record all supplies pulled from inventory in the inventory log?	determine how many supplies not recorded in term of dollar amount
Does the sales supervisor correctly classify sales by state that subject the business to sale taxes?	dollar amount correctly identifying tax liability
What is the percentage of sales are subject to sales tax due to tax authority relative to total sales?	If the analyst asks the question, "Is the percentage 20% of all transactions", attribute sampling could be used. But here the auditor also may want to know the dollar volume.
What percentage of supplies are pulled from inventory subject to sale promotion deduction each month?	Analyst wants to be able to match sales transaction count and volume with recorded cost of goods sold?
What percentage of expenses have been properly recorded for a federal research tax credit.	The analysts wants to know how many and the dollar amount that qualifies for tax credits

The examples above are concerned with the primary question being, how much (dollar volume)? However dollars do not operate in a vacuum. There are always subsidiary personnel, client and organizational issues that need to be explored. Let's take the example of a medical claims adjudication case. In addition to determining the dollar error rate there should also be an examination of attributes as they relate to specific staff and claim types, medical office structure and health plan design characteristics. The auditor starts with an assessment of dollar volume slippage in the system but from that point one has to determine which attributes should be followed up. The attributes therefore provide the basis for the detective work required to make system corrections.

In forecasting revenue and expenses there are several attributes that are of importance. Attributes such as age, gender, location and other sociodemographic characteristics. This will be discussed in more detail in Part II.

Sampling and Uncertainty – In most circumstances sampling always involves uncertainty. One has to consider the possibility that any calculation of our decision target value can result from sampling error. That error can be caused by an unrepresentative sample by chance that can lead to incorrect targeting values.

This is termed a Type I Misstatement. The probability of committing a Type I error in the statistical literature is also called alpha error. Alternatively, the audit population we are interested may actually meet our targeted standard, but by random chance we draw a sample that show no targets met. This is a Type II misstatement. The probability of committing a Type II error is known as beta error. Type II errors may occur because the actual target amount (the "effect size") is small and the variability in our samples obscures the ability to detect it.

You can guard against committing a Type I error by using an appropriately small alpha level, say, 0.05 or lower. In calculating sample size Auditmetrics uses 5% for type I error. Exactly what are the dynamics of this statistical targeting process? Let's start with a simple example. Suppose it is proposed that with the flip of a coin I set up a wager, if heads I would be paid a certain dollar amount but if tails I pay out. Of course it is a bet that in the long run should be a net zero to each because the Probability of heads would be 50%. It is better odds than at a casino that always favors the house. It is the excitement of a long run of good luck or a large wager with a big return.

Is my game of chance a valid proposal or is the coin a fake that will favor me? So I will let you do a statistical sample tossing of the coin five times.

Since the flip of a coin has a dichotomous outcome, 1- heads 2- tails, the binomial distribution can be used to calculate the probability of all of the possible outcomes of five tosses of the coin:

No. Heads	Probability
0	3.10%
1	15.60%
2	31.30%
3	31.30%
4	15.60%
5	3.10%

An outcome of all heads or tails is 3.10 %. If our target alpha standard is $p \leq 5\%$ and if the outcome after five flips is all heads, that is rare enough for a conclusion that the coin may be biased favoring heads. The decision no deal, the coin is biased. Can that be a mistaken decision? Yes.

If the coin turns out to be unbiased then the conclusion is incorrect? If that happens then we are committing an alpha error. In more traditional statistical terminology, a true "null hypothesis" of a fair coin has been rejected. The null hypothesis is that there is no difference between the sampled coin and a true unbiased coin. When that hypothesis was rejected, an alpha error was committed.

Guarding against a Type II error is more problematic. A test that will detect differences if it exists, regardless of population variability, is said to have high statistical power. Since Power = 1 −beta, and a low beta (probability of missing an important target) equates to a high power of the test. **Statistical power is directly related to sample size.** The larger the sample size (n) the tighter the precision.

Hypothesis Testing – The Auditmetrics AI methodology tests samples by comparing sample estimates with audit population values. It uses the power of the computer to test in real time any number of sample estimates to determine if standards such as precision are met. Immediate feedback allows one to resample if targets are not met.

Assisted AI works because a selected sample can be compared with values from the book that are known through accounting system reports. But, what if we don't know the audit population parameters? This is the usual case in the realm of statistical inference. Whether doing market research or randomized clinical trials in medical research, the usual case is that the population parameters such and means and totals are unknown. The sample is the only means to project population values. This process requires a testing mechanism with clearly defined starting assumptions.

All textbooks talk about the "null hypothesis. In inferential statistics, the null hypothesis is a general statement or default position that there is nothing significantly different happening, like there is no association among groups or variables, or that there is no difference between two measured phenomena. Testing (accepting or rejecting) the null hypothesis helps in concluding that there is (or is not) grounds for believing that there is a relationship between two phenomena.

The null hypothesis can be described as "academic conservativism". For example in testing a new randomized drug trial the starting point is to assume the drug does not provide a measurable improvement in

37

clinical performance, the classical null hypothesis. Any difference between experimental and control subjects is due to random fluctuation and not a "treatment effect". From this starting point, statistical evidence is used to disprove this initial assumption. The intent is to favor the decision not to accept the bad outcome of introducing an ineffective therapy. It is preferable to reject a therapy that may be effective. This is a philosophical judgement. When a hypothesis is rejected there is usually a follow up. So the wheel keeps turning to find a solution. Eventually the false rejection will be corrected with ongoing research.

The more insidious error is beta error. This is when a false null hypothesis is accepted. This leads to a dynamic that there is a false sense of there is nothing there. Researchers will turn to other fruitful endeavors when the original case should not have been closed.

How does this conservatism affect an accountant doing an internal Audit? What is the cost of an alpha error? If an auditor rejects a book value, the tendency is to increase sample size or search for additional evidence to show that the book is misstated. Additional work may reverse the original decision or support it. On the other hand, if the auditor accepts an actual misstated book value, beta error, generally there is a sense of stability and not a need to seek further data. That is the insidious nature of beta risk, a misstatement that can linger. Sample size reduces beta risk but there is a trade of sample size and cost. Auditmetrics reduces beta error by performing several iterations cross referencing actual book values.

Auditmetrics AI Hypothesis Testing – Auditmetrics generates two Excel templates that contain statistical inference testing algorithms. The purpose of this testing is to accept the sample or put it aside and select a new sample. Some inferences follow more traditional methods and others use specialized AI assist methods in drawing conclusions. One such specialized test is whether the estimate of total book value from the random sample matches the margin of error initially set in the calculation of sample size. This AI assistance method uses computer algorithms in testing if sample margin of error of the original design is actually represented in the selected sample. If the test is not met a new sample is drawn until the test is passed.

An issue can arise if "what if the total book value is not known"? Then more traditional methods of statistical inference must be employed. It is worthwhile to examine those methods because auditors who desire to be expert in statistical auditing must have them as part of their armamentarium.

Summary

An often-heard statement is that "Statistics has proved such and such." There is of course also the even stronger statement that "Statistics can prove anything." In fact, having examined the structure of statistical logic, it should be clear that one does not "prove" anything. Rather, one is looking at consistency or inconsistency between the observed data and a proposed hypotheses.

If the observed data is "consistent" with the null hypothesis then instead of "proving the hypothesis true," the proper interpretation is that there is no reason to doubt that the null hypothesis is true.

Goal III – Model Building

In statistics, a model is a mathematical equation that describes a functional relationship between two or more variables. A basic model is the regression model. It is a mathematical equation that relates a dependent variable and one or more independent variables. The simplest mathematical equation that can be used for model building is linear regression.

In essence past data is used to predict future outcomes. The assumption is that the pattern of past data will likely continue in the future. The ability to use regression to model economic situations and predict future outcomes make regression models extremely powerful business tool. The power of regression models contribute to their popularity in economics, business and finance.

However, markets and business climates can exhibit unanticipated volatility. The key for survival is to constantly monitor data trends. It is usual for a business to see a certain amount of regularity in its data. But markets can suddenly change. If a business constantly samples it accounts, it will have an excellent chance of detecting new trends before being overwhelmed. Broadly speaking, market volatility measures the amount of deviation away from the average. Volatility is also the rate of change of deviations over time.

The ability of the regression model to accurately predict future trends depends on the strength the relationship between the independent and the dependent variables. The model can only be as good as the quality of the data that is used to build it. The most efficient strategy is to sample accounts on a regular basis. Regular management reports my hide those subtle changes that may be indicators of future unanticipated changes. Regular statistically valid sampling allows for timely and efficient detailed account analysis to find trends that may be hidden in standard accounting computerized reports.

The linear Model

One way to determine the volatility of the relationship between dependent and independent variables is by computing the correlation coefficient. If the correlation shows a strong relationship (closer to 1, irrespective of the sign), then one can be comfortable with the current model. The gradual degradation of correlation is a sign that other inputs are becoming more important and that the current independent/dependent variable model must be re-examined. This may be the first sign major changes are under way.

The simplest linear model is the **bivariate model**:

- Have a set of data with two variables, X and Y.

- The goal is to find a simple, convenient mathematical function that explains the relationship between X and Y.

Suppose dollars spent on advertising is plotted against increase in sales as shown in the following graphical representation:

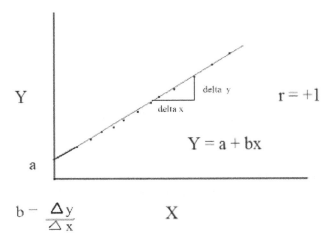

This example is a plot of the amount of money spent on advertising (X) with an increase in total sales (Y). This mathematical model is a linear function where b is the slope of the line also called the regression coefficient and a is the Y intercept which is the value of Y when X is zero. In this example all data points follow a straight line. The data fit the linear model perfectly, therefore the correlation (r) is 1. It is a perfect model with X being the independent variable and Y the dependent variable. If we know X we can therefore perfectly predict Y.

This plot is an example of a direct relationship between X and Y, as X goes up so does Y. There can also be an inverse relationship between X and Y. For example if X is price and Y total sales the following plot examines this mathematical relationship.

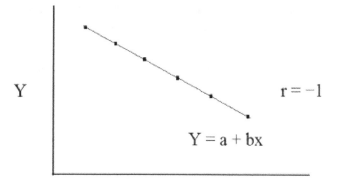

Y = a + bx

r = -1

X

Raise price then total sales go down. This plot is an example of an inverse relationship but it should be note the real world relationship between price and demand can be very complex. It depends on "price elasticity" of demand on how sensitive price is to the demand for a particular good or service and the possibility of substitution of other goods and services.

The examples so far reflect a world where our model is perfect. All data points fit the mathematical function perfectly. What would a complete lack of functional relationship between our X and Y look like?

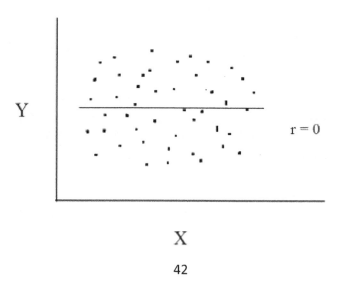

r = 0

X

This is an example of a zero correlation indicating no functional relationship between X and Y. At each level of X there are both high and low values of Y. But useful real world data is somewhere between the previous extreme scenarios. For example:

Scatter Plot

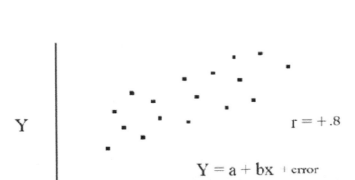

Y

$r = +.8$

$Y = a + bx$ ǀ error

X

Most real world data does not perfectly follow mathematical functions, BUT is the data fit good enough? In this example there is a general trend, as X increases so does Y. We can fit a straight line to summarize the functional relationship to make projections. However around that line is a zone of uncertainty. The linear function in this example contains an error value. Measuring statistical error was presented previously with the discussion of standard deviation around the mean

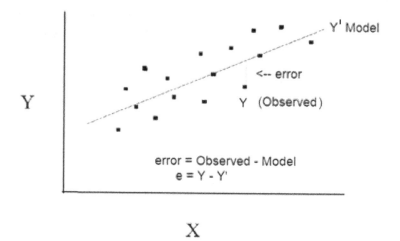

The line depicted above is what is termed the "best fit line". One could manually place a plot of a straight line that appears to be a good fit of the data. Y' is the straight line (Y' = a + bx) which is our mathematical model while Y is each individual observed data point. To obtain maximum statistical efficiency is to mathematically derive a straight line that minimizes the deviations (Y-Y') around the prediction model.

Standard deviation discussed in the section on descriptive statistics is a measure of the spread of individual data points around the mean. In this case the measure of spread is data points around the straight line. The error measure (e) outlined in the graph is the deviation of each data point. The key is to find a line that minimizes deviations around the straight line:

Minimize $(e)^2$ =least square line

The formula's goal is to minimize the square of the deviations around the line. Why the square of the deviations? It is the same reason why to first calculate variance around the means since deviation above and below the mean cancel out to zero. In the least square line all deviations above the line will cancel out those below and add to zero. The formula is:

$$S^2{}_{x.y} = \frac{\Sigma(e)^2}{n-2}$$

The formula measures the variance around the regression line. Since we will be working with a sample of the data, the formula is the square of the deviations around the line divided by the degrees of freedom (df). In the standard deviation around the mean, degrees of freedom is n-1. When you draw a sample one observation is needed to start fixing the mean and the rest are free to vary. With this formula two data points are needed to start fixing a straight line, the rest are free to vary.

Mathematical methods of minimizing the square deviations around the straight line is accomplished by using differential calculus minima/maxima calculations. With the regression straight line:

$$Y' = a + bX$$

the formulas for A intercept and B slope minimizes error around the straight line:

$$b = \frac{n\Sigma xy - (\Sigma x)(\Sigma y)}{n(\Sigma x^2) - (\Sigma x)^2}$$

$$a = \bar{y} - b\bar{x}$$

We now have the ingredients to start to use regression, sometimes referred to as ordinary least squares (OLS), as a tool in predicting future economic performance based on historical data.

Error distribution around the regression line

We have discussed the nature of the random process and the role of the normal curve. The error term for the regression line is based on the assumption that the errors are randomly distributed as displayed below:

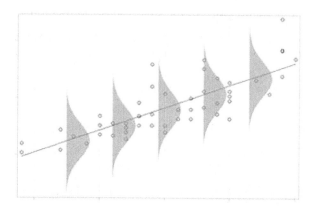

- The error term may assume any positive, negative or zero value and is a random variable.

- The mean value of the error term is zero (mean(e) = 0).

- The variance of the error is constant at any given value of X.

- The error has a normal distribution with a variance of $S^2y.x$

Part II – Forecasting Revenue and Expenses Using Regression

Forecasting business revenue and expenses is as much art as science. Many business managers complain that building forecasts with any degree of accuracy takes a lot of time. It is better spent selling rather than planning. But few financial institutions will put money in a business if it's unable to provide a set of thoughtful forecasts. More important, proper financial forecasts will help develop operational and staffing plans that will help make a business more efficient.

Correlation and regression are powerful statistical tools that can be used for forecasting revenue and expenses. The key is to draw random samples from relevant accounts. Appendix I covers how to draw a stratified random sample using Excel. Though using Excel is a great convenience it is somewhat tedious and only practical when sampling relatively small accounts. The book available at **Amazon**:

"Statistical Audit Automation"

covers how to use the Auditmetrics® AI system to draw random samples. The AI assisted software prepares business managers to conduct statistical audits that are mathematically efficient, inexpensive and easy to use. Just as in political polling, the starting point is to set a targeted margin of error and the software then guides the user to the drawing of a fully validated and documented random sample.

Financial Projections

Most business planners would prefer making revenue forecasts, it's easy to forget about expenses. Many will optimistically focus on reaching revenue goals and assume expenses can be adjusted to accommodate the incoming revenue. In this section is discussed using regression and correlation to forecast both revenue and expenses. It is my experience when preparing a business plan, start with expenses. Most small business fail because costs are inadequately defined and controlled. The best way to reconcile revenue and expense projections is by a series of reality checks for key ratios. Here are a few ratios that should help as a guide:

Gross margin. It's the ratio of total direct costs to total revenue during a given quarter or given year? This is one of the areas in which aggressive assumptions typically become too unrealistic. Beware of assumptions that make your gross margin increase from 10 to 50 percent.

Operating profit margin. It's the ratio of total operating costs--direct costs and fixed cost overheard, excluding financing costs--to total revenue during a given time period. A growing business should show a positive movement with this ratio. As revenues grow, overhead costs should represent a small proportion of total costs. When developing a business plan regression analysis is a valuable tool in developing projections of both revenue and expenses. Building an accurate set of growth projections for a startup will take time but regression statistical tools will help paying attention to detail and expedite the process.

Revenue Projections Using Regression

Scenario #1: Projecting Monthly Revenue

This projection will use 3 years (36 months) of sales data. The data was from a small business so we did not have to use a random sample. It is fine up to a point but account data with large volume of transactions such as greater than 10,000 records it may be valuable to select a random sample.

Below is an excerpt of the an account that record a company's sales data:

Month	year	month	sales	yhat	Residual
1	1	Jan	$129,646	$70,216	-$59,430
2	1	Feb	$126,227	$84,814	-$41,413
3	1	March	$151,966	$99,412	-$52,554
4	1	April	$165,168	$114,011	-$51,157
5	1	May	$182,977	$128,609	-$54,368
6	1	June	$145,694	$143,207	-$2,487
7	1	July	$156,814	$157,805	$991
8	1	August	$150,373	$172,404	$22,031
9	1	September	$146,155	$187,002	$40,847
10	1	October	$202,621	$201,600	-$1,021
11	1	November	$217,081	$216,198	-$883
12	1	December	$222,458	$230,797	$8,339
13	2	January	$198,338	$245,395	$47,057
"	"	"	"	"	"

The model to project sales is:

Y = a +bX + error where Y is total sales and X is the month count

Y = (Model) + error as measured by $S^2y.x$; model is the linear function

In terms of the account variables: Projected Sales = a + b(Month)

Excel can be used to calculate the values of intercept (a) and slope (b) that minimizes $S^2y.x$ which is sometimes referred to as <u>residual error</u>. The error term in this model are the variables that are unknown and not measured.

Excel Professional that includes the "Analysis Toolpak" must be installed separately, it is not automatically installed when Excel. This is accomplished when a workbook is open, going to file select -> options and then select "add ins" then Analysis Toolpak. What you will then see as you click on data "data analysis" on the menu:

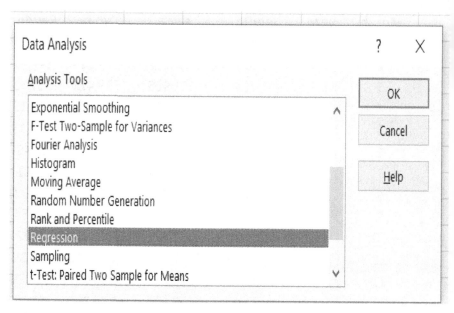

Select Regression and the following window will pop up:

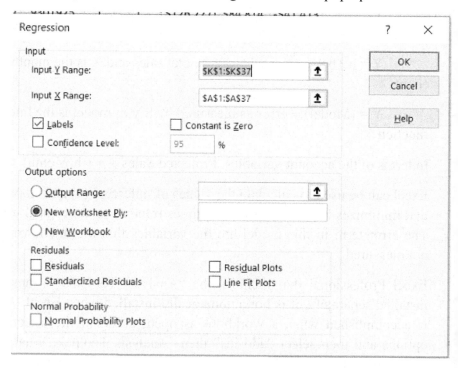

Input Y range is the sales variable and X range is the month number. Since "Labels" is checked the columns selected include the top cell that indicates variable names. You notice the default confidence interval is 95%. There is no need to change 95%, it is also the default for the Auditmetrics® sample selection.

The Regression results will be output to a new spread sheet. Below is an excerpt of the most relevant portions of the results:

SUMMARY OUTPUT

Regression Statistics	
R	0.95
R Square	0.91
Adjusted R Square	0.91
Standard Error	47809
Observations	36

	Coefficient	Standard Error	t Stat	P-value
Intercept	55617	16274.25419	3.417518	0.0000
Month	14598	767.0336696	19.0321	0.0000

In our model a = $ 55,617 and b = $14,598

The formula becomes: Sales = $55,617 + $14,598 x Month. The p value is the alpha error that was discussed in the section on statistical inference. To reject the null hypothesis the usual standard is alpha <= .05. The P-value of 0.0000 means it is so small that we can reject the null hypothesis and therefore conclude that the regression line is not due to random fluctuation. A more valuable value to determine is the "goodness of fit" of the model to the data is R^2 which will be explained later.

Now let us look at a plot of the trend:

Sales by Month

As displayed above: the straight line is sales = a + b x (Month). The correlation is .95 which means the data is a good fit. A better measure of the fit is R^2. Its formal definition is the **percentage of the variance of Y that is explained by X**. We have discussed the variance around the regression line is $S^2x.y$ and the variance around the mean of Y is S^2y.

Month	month	Y (Sales)	Predicted Y'	Residual (Y'-Y)
1	Jan	$129,646	$70,216	-$59,430
2	Feb	$126,227	$84,814	-$41,413
3	March	$151,966	$99,412	-$52,554
4	April	$165,168	$114,011	-$51,157
5	May	$182,977	$128,609	-$54,368
6	June	$145,694	$143,207	-$2,487
7	July	$156,814	$157,805	$991
8	August	$150,373	$172,404	$22,031
9	September	$146,155	$187,002	$40,847
10	October	$202,621	$201,600	-$1,021
11	November	$217,081	$216,198	-$883
12	December	$222,458	$230,797	$8,339
13	Jan	198338	245395	47057
"	"	"	"	"

The data above is sales data with an added two columns: Predicted Y' which is the linear formula. If you plot this column using Excel a straight line would be the result. The residual is the error, the difference between the straight line and actual data point (Y'-Y). The standard deviation of the of the residual:

> Where e = (Y'-Y) follows the normal distribution with a mean of 0

$$S_{y.x} = \sqrt{\frac{\Sigma(e)^2}{n-2}}$$

$S_{x.y}$ can be calculated by the Excel formula for standard deviation of the residual column:

$$S_{x.y} = STDEV.S(M2:M37) = \$47,121$$

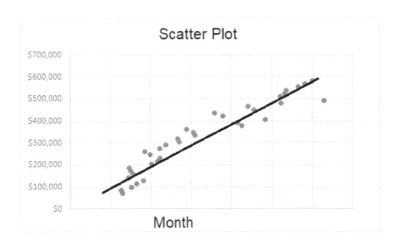

The scatter plot displays the spread of data around the regression line which is measured by standard deviation. This indicates a relatively good fit. R^2 of .91 means 91% of the variance of Y (sales) is explained by the model that uses month as a predictor.

Example: *a display the concept of R^2. Suppose we have an account Y but we don't have any knowledge of an X to build a model. Then the best predictor of Y is the mean of Y. Let's use an example with a Y that has a **mean of 90** and a **variance around the mean is 4** and a standard deviation of 2. If we do not have an X predictor the best predictor of future Y is the mean 90 with a variance of 4 which represents our uncertainty.*

Y (sales) is only variable known:

Mean = 90 is the best predictor

Variance: S^2_y = 4 (uncertainty)

Both X and Y Known but with prefect prediction R = 1

$S^2_{y.x}$ = 0 no error around regression line

$R^2 = 1-(S^2_{y.x}/S^2_y) = 1-(0/4) = 1$ or 100% Y variance explained

This is a scenario where our mathematical model is perfect and fully explains all the data points. The variance around the regression line is zero. Therefore all the deviations of the data points around the mean of Y are explained by X.

Both X and Y Known and R = .8

S^2_{yx} = 1.44

$R^2 = 1-(S^2_{yx}/S^2_y) = 1-(1.44/4) = 1-.36$

R^2 = .64 or 64% of Y variance explained

Some fields of study have an inherently greater amount of unexplainable variation. In those cases, R^2 values are bound to be lower. For example, studies that try to explain human behavior generally have R^2 values of less than 50%. People are just harder to predict than things like physical processes and account activity. In accounting and busines, the models are processes that can vary but in a well-run business, profits and losses must at some point be somewhat predictable. So generally business forecasts should have an R^2 50% or greater.

Scenario #2: Multiple Regression

So far our basic model is a bi-variate linear model, a dependent variable and only one predictor variable. Though we have a very good fit there is a problem with our model so far. Data is that of a wholesaler that supplies retail outlets. So if we make a prediction for the next month or quarter it will always be higher than the previous month or quarter. But business activity does have seasonal fluctuations. The fourth quarter of the year with its holiday activity will always be higher than the following first quarter of the following year. The model as it exists does not allow for seasonal fluctuations.

We need a new model with two predictor variables that includes monthly and quarterly predictors using multiple regression. It is a statistical technique that uses several explanatory variables to predict the outcome of a response variable. The goal of multiple linear regression is to model the linear relationship between the explanatory (independent) variables and response (dependent) variable. In essence, multiple regression is an extension of ordinary least-squares (OLS) regression that involves more than one explanatory variable.

Simple and Multiple Linear Regression

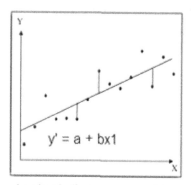

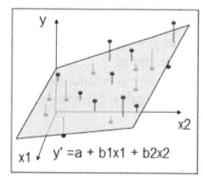

In simple linear regression the least-squares estimators minimize the sum of the squared errors from the estimated regression line.

In multiple linear regression the least-squares estimators minimize the sum of the squared errors from the estimated regression plane.

Setting Up Data to Adjust for Seasonal Fluctuations

The first step is to determine whether if there is indeed seasonal fluctuation and then set up the data file for such adjustment. If there is evidence of fluctuations, the next step is to set up the data file with a quarterly input matrix. The first step is to use an excel pivot table to break down sales data by quarter. If quarterly fluctuations are detected then set up a regression input matrix with quarterly inputs.

Below is the data matrix that we will use to determine and adjust for quarterly fluctuations:

Month	month	quarter	sales	Q1	Q2	Q3
1	Jan	1	$129,646	1	0	0
2	Feb	1	$126,227	1	0	0
3	March	1	$151,966	1	0	0
4	April	2	$165,168	0	1	0
5	May	2	$182,977	0	1	0
6	June	2	$145,694	0	1	0
7	July	3	$156,814	0	0	1

8	August	3	$150,373	0	0	1
9	September	3	$146,155	0	0	1
10	October	4	$202,621	0	0	0
11	November	4	$217,081	0	0	0
12	December	4	$222,458	0	0	0
13	Jan	1	198338	1	0	0
"	"	"	"	"	"	"

First let's determine if there is evidence of seasonal fluctuations. Make sure in the data the variables of interest are contiguous.

1. Use Excel Pivot Table to perform data breakdown by quarter

2. Go to insert at the menu at the top

3. Select Pivot Chart in the Charts section:

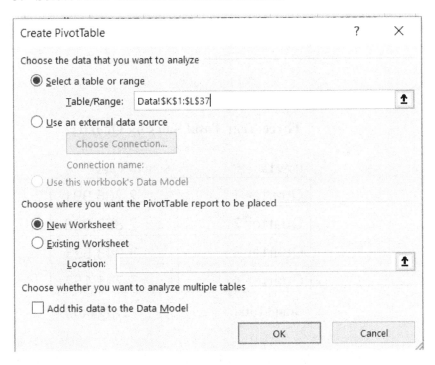

The Table/Range is the shaded area of the data matrix and below are the settings for the following pivot table.

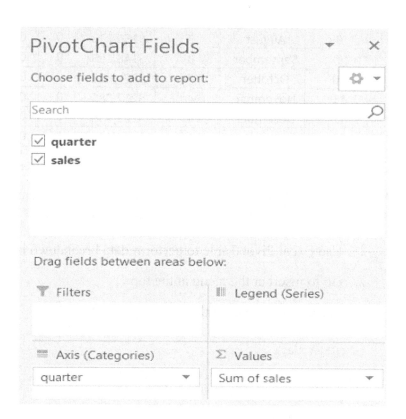

Three Year Total Sales by Quarter:

Row Labels	Sum of sales
Quarter 1	2,206,991
Quarter 2	2,863,008
Quarter 3	2,943,523
Quarter 4	3,711,152
Grand Total	**11,724,674**

As can be seen, there is clear indication of quarterly fluctuation of total sales.

Setting Up Quarterly Input Variables

Dummy Variables: A special attribute variable in statistics and econometrics, particularly in regression analysis, is one that takes only the value 0 or 1. It indicates the absence or presence of some categorical effect that is expected to shift the outcome. They can be thought of as numeric stand-ins for qualitative facts in a regression model, sorting data into mutually exclusive categories (such as men and woman).

In the case of quarterly adjustments we set up the data matrix with the following dummy variables:

- Quarter 1 – 1 if yes or 0 if no

- Quarter 2 – 1 if yes or 0 if no

- Quarter 3 – 1 if yes or 0 if no

You may notice the data matrix has dummies for three of the four quarters. It may seem logical to set up four like below:

Q1 0,1
Q2 0,1
Q3 0,1
Q4 0,1

The problem with this scheme is that the last dummy variable (Q4) is redundant. If the first three dummy variables are 0 then it is a given that **Q4 has to be 1**. So the rule is:

1. The number of dummy variables necessary to represent a single attribute variable is equal to the number of levels (categories) in that variable minus one.

2. For a given attribute variable, none of the dummy variables constructed can be redundant. That is, one dummy variable

cannot be a constant multiple, simple linear relation or dfined by another.

In the multiple regression formula the predicted value for Quarter 4 is when Quarter 1 to Quarter 3 are all Zero.

Using Excel Function to set up dummy variables

Rather than manually entering dummy values one can program entries using Excel's =if function. Like every function and formula in Excel, IF is based on a specific syntax:

$$=IF(condition, value\ if\ true, value\ if\ false)$$

As shown above, the function has three parameters, the first two of which are compulsory.

Condition: This position must contain a condition – a comparison between two values – where one or both values can be cell references. The possible conditions are:
Equal (=)
Unequal (<>)
Less than (<)
Greater than (>)
Less than or equal to (<=)
Greater than or equal to (>=)

Below is the data matrix displaying the formula in the first row:

	A	B	C	D
1	Quarter	Q1	Q2	Q3
2	1	=if(a2=1,1,0)	=if(a2=2,1,0)	=if(a2=3,1,0)
3	1	1	0	0
4	1	1	0	0
5	2	0	1	0
6	2	0	1	0
7	2	0	1	0
8	3	0	0	1
9	3	0	0	1
10	3	0	0	1
11	4	0	0	0
12	4	0	0	0
13	4	0	0	0
14	1	1	0	0
15	"	"	"	"

The Full Regression Equation

The multiple linear equation with quarterly dummies now becomes:

Total Sales = $83,049 + ($14,317 x Month)

+ (-$38,272 x $Q1_{dummy}$)

+ (-$8,334 x $Q2_{dummy}$)

+ (-$42,340 x $Q3_{dummy}$)

Let's now project the estimated total sales for Month 36, Quarter 4 and Month 37 Quarter 1:

Total Sales Month 36 = $83,049 + ($14,317 x 36) = $598,461

Total Sales Month 37 = $83,049 + ($14,317 x 37) + (1 x -$38,272)= $574,506

As expected quarter 1 projection is lower than previous 4th quarter value.

Limitations of Regression in Forecasting

Past data is used to predict future outcomes. Since our data has excellent R^2, prediction can be very reliable but up to a point. To understand what this means we should be aware that any statistical projection does have a certain amount of error. The regression line does have a 95% confidence interval band. Like any statistical estimate the line has a band of uncertainty. The 95% means that out of 100 samples, 95 would be within the band that contains the population's true value while 5 would be outside that band. Those prediction outside would represent a 5% alpha error as discussed in the section on statistical inference.

The confidence interval around a mean is a straight forward constant interval around the mean. However, the confidence interval bands around the prediction line is more complex. The exhibit below depicts the 95% confidence interval around the regression line:

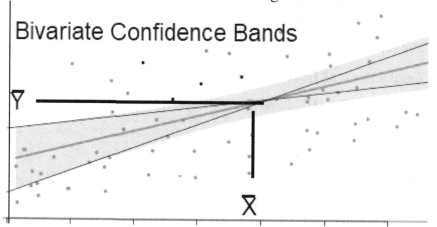

The band of confidence is the narrowest at the intersection of the means of the constituent variables. For example for two variables the best prediction is at the intersection of the two means. As you go up the X scale the bands expand and predictions have steady wider confidence intervals. It is not that much of a problem with a model with a good fit of R^2 to project two or three quarters in the future. Maybe a year if the database of the regression is of sufficient size. Projecting over 12 months based on six month of data will have unstable estimates.

As the new quarterly regression data is added to the database it is best to drop and archive the earliest quarter. This keeps the data current. This is a way to start detecting any degradation of the model such as R^2 slipping which may be an indication of shifts in the market that may need further analysis.

Using Regression to measure impact of demographics

Regression is very valuable in adjusting predictions using categorical adjustments for various demographics such as geographic region and other characteristics such as gender. Geographic region can also be a surrogate for income distribution which is readily available from government published data. For example there is available through IRS sources income tax collections by zip code. Such data combined with census population data by zip is a good surrogate for socio economic characteristics. With a little care many other indicators of socioeconomic significance can be collected.

Below is a data set that incorporates geographic areas based on zip codes:

Zip_Code	Zip_Area	Sales
0017	1	3,102
0016	1	6,658
0008	1	6,514
0012	1	10,000
0007	1	6,000
0005	1	9,634
0011	1	12,666
0003	2	35,548
0006	2	40,508
0020	2	60,074
"	"	"

The Regression line results:

	Coefficients	Standard Error	t Stat	P-value
Intercept	-$30,885	$6,135	-5.0	0000
Zip_Area	$47,049	$2,540	18.5	.0000

Sales = -$30,885 + $47,049 x Zip Area

Area	Sum of Sales
Zip Area 1	$185,228
Zip Area 2	$446,808
Zip Area 3	$608,160
Zip Area 4	$602,265
Grand Total	**$1,842,461**

As part of small business forecasting, it is key to get a picture of the possibilities for selling your products or services in a local market. Looking at a local markets will provide information about the types of people who might buy products or services and how far is the company's geographic reach, and what is the competition within that market area.

Step One: Determining Market Area

Before doing research on local markets, you will need to know the size of that market. The question to ask yourself is: "How far will people come to buy my products or services?" The answer depends upon two factors: (a) the type of products provided, and (b) the availability of similar businesses (in other words, competitors).

Step Two: Create a Profile of the Ideal Customer

Next, you need to figure out who are the people who will buy your products or services.

What age are they?

What is their income level?

What is their education level?

What does their family look like?

What kind of jobs do they have?

What do they like to do for entertainment?

It may be too cumbersome and difficult for a small business to survey for such data. But a focus group is a small demographically diverse group of people whose reactions are studied especially in market research or political analysis. It is set up in guided or open discussions about new products or current views of the company to determine reactions that can be expected from a larger population. The use of focus groups is a market research method that is intended to collect data through interactive and directed discussions by a researcher. If there are issues with lagging sales that don't respond to standard means of marketing then arranging for a focus group may be what is needed.

Controlling Expenses Using Regression and Correlation

Below is some detail on how to go about building financial forecasts especially when starting a learning curve. When beginning the process of forecasting, start with expenses, not revenues. It's much easier to forecast expenses than revenues. So start with estimates for the most common categories of expenses as follows:

Fixed Costs/Overhead:	Variable Costs
Indirect labor cost	Cost of goods sold
Utility bills	Materials and supplies
Phone bills/communication costs	Packaging
Rent	Direct labor costs
Utility bills	Customer service
Accounting/bookkeeping	Direct sales cost
Legal/insurance/licensing fees	Direct marketing cost
Postage	
Technology	
Advertising & marketing	

The Variable Budget

A variable budget, also called Flexible budget, is a financial plan of estimated expenses based on a measure of current amount of customer activity. In other words, a variable budget uses the expenses produced in the current production of goods and services as a baseline to estimate how expenses will change based on changes in customer activity. Management often uses variable budgets before a period to predict both a best and worst case scenario for the upcoming accounting period. This provides a "what if" look at the future of the company's financial performance. Correlation analysis is also used as a measure as to how well expenses are controlled.

Below is an example of 12 month data linked to output as measured by contracts signed.

Contracts Signed	Cost of Goods	Direct Labor	Other	Fixed Cost
3000	$14,500	$24,500	$21,000	$75,000
3800	$16,700	$31,400	$26,000	$75,000
5000	$20,000	$33,500	$31,500	$75,000
5800	$21,500	$38,700	$35,000	$75,000
4100	$14,050	$29,300	$24,100	$75,000
3100	$15,900	$26,600	$22,500	$75,000
3200	$20,100	$26,500	$22,500	$75,000
4800	$19,900	$24,100	$29,400	$75,000
4500	$17,900	$30,000	$28,600	$75,000
3700	$15,000	$29,100	$26,000	$75,000
5100	$22,500	$36,700	$32,000	$75,000
6000	$23,010	$39,500	$35,000	$75,000

In this budget:

1. Contracts signed is the measure of customer activity in delivering specified goods and services.

2. Cost of goods is a variable cost that includes goods cost including materials and supplies that are associated with the delivery of the goods.

3. Direct labor is labor costs associated with the delivery of the goods and services.

4. Other is the catch-all that includes customer service and marketing costs.

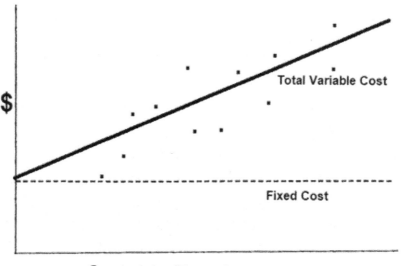

Contracts Signed

This is a plot of all variable cost as they relate to the output measure, contracts signed. Fixed cost are constant and do not vary with output (contracts signed).This is a good overview but in order to control expenses we must look at each individual variable cost and determine how closely each is associated with output. To do this we will use correlation as the measure of the association of each variable cost as it relates to output.

Correlation Results:

X- Independent Variable -> Signed Contracts

Y – Dependent Variables:

- Cost of Goods
- Direct Labor
- Other Expenses

	Cost of Goods	Direct Labor	Other
(correlation) R=	0.77	0.82	0.98
(slope) B=	$2.38	$4.22	$4.66

We could have done regression projections and do what if scenarios but for now it is essential if our variable costs are under control. It is variable cost that should have a more or less direct relationship with output. A look at R^2 would give a better picture of goodness of fit and a measure of cost control. The R^2 are as follows: Cost of Goods 59%, Direct Labor 67% and other expenses 96%. Other expenses including marketing and customer service are efficient as they relate to output. A good target for the other expenses is to reach a R^2 of 75%. Top priority is to examine all costs associated with cost of goods which is not just cost of goods but also materials and packaging.

The Variable Budget:

Aveage Signed Contracts/Month	2,917	4,167	5,000	6,250
Annual Contracts	35,000	50,000	60,000	75,000
Fixed	$75,000	$75,000	$75,000	$75,000
Cost of Goods	$83,442	$119,203	$143,043	$178,804
Direct Labor	$147,865	$211,236	$253,483	$316,854
Other Expenses	$34,276	$232,888	$279,465	$349,331
Total Budget	$340,583	$688,327	$750,991	$919,989
Budget: monthly regression formula X 12 for annual budget				

Companies develop a budget based on their expectations for their most likely level of sales and expenses. They can use their various expected levels of production to create a variable budget that include different levels of production. Then, they can modify the variable budget when they have their actual production volume and compare it to the variable budget for the same production volume. A variable budget is more complicated, requires a solid understanding of a company's fixed and variable expenses, and allows for greater control over changes that occur throughout the year.

Example: *suppose a proposed sale of items does not occur because the large volume expected client A opted to go with another supplier. In a static budget situation, this would result in large variances in many accounts due to the fixed budget being set based on sales that included large client. A variable budget would allow management to adjust their expectations of the budget for both changes in costs and revenue that would occur from the loss of the client. The changes made in the variable budget would then be compared to what actually* *occurs to result in more realistic and representative variance. This ability to change the budget also makes it easier to pinpoint who is responsible if a revenue or cost target is missed.*

Non Linear Functions

One of the most common questions asked about regression is how sure are you that the straight line is the best model for forecasting revenue and controlling costs? Before going forth with analysis it is always wise to plot the data and determine if the data does indeed seem to follow a linear function. Below is a plot of long term dynamics of the start-up, growth phase and eventual slowing down of growth though a business would try to avoid this phase.

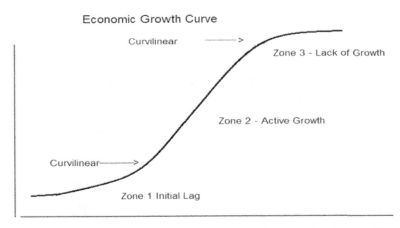

Displayed is a long term growth curve for any business. There is an initial investment and a lag (zone 1) in growth leading to the start of accelerated growth (zone 2) . Linear regression would be a good fit for zone 2. Zone 1 is not a good fit for linear regression but there are other regression options that can be used.

Zone 1 is the critical phase in the growth curve. To obtain investment a careful examination of expenses and projected revenue is paramount. Below is a graph of a proposed start up cash flow:

Graph: A linear model would not be a good fit.

Monthly Cash Flow

Proposed Function $= Y = e^{x}$

Monthly Break Even

Table:

Exponent	Month	Monthly
0.25	1	$1,284
0.5	2	$1,649
0.75	3	$2,117
1	4	$2,718
1.25	5	$3,490
1.5	6	$4,482
1.75	7	$5,755
2	8	$7,389
2.25	9	**$9,488**
2.5	10	$12,182
2.75	11	$15,643
3	12	$20,086

Based on planning research the monthly breakeven point where cash inflow equals cash outflow is $10,000 which is around month 9. The monthly cash flow in the last column follows a classic initial lagged growth which is $Y' = e^X$:

Exponent	Month	Monthly
=0.25	1	=EXP(D5) *1000
=D5+0.25	2	=EXP(D6) *1000

The exponents are selected to set up a reasonable cash flow projection. The Excel function =EXP(month) generates the exponential function e^X. This is a theoretical projection but as we collect the actual cash flow data can we use regression to measure how well the theoretical data matches the actual observed cash flow data. Excel Regression will not fit well with observed cash flow if it follows a curvilinear growth pattern. But the data can be transformed to by converting dollars to the natural log of the dollars. The Excel natural log function is =ln(Cash).

Month	Monthly Cash	Natural Log
1	$1,284	7.16
2	$1,649	7.41
3	$2,117	7.66
4	$2,718	7.91
5	$3,490	8.16
6	$4,482	8.41
7	$5,755	8.66
8	$7,389	8.91
9	$9,488	9.16
10	$12,182	9.41
11	$15,643	9.66
12	$20,086	9.91

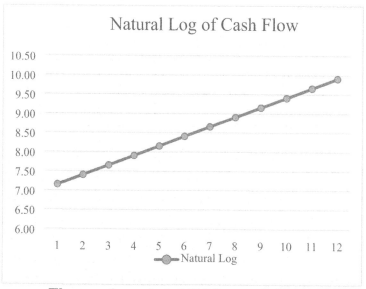

Natural Log of Cash Flow

The new formula is LN(Y) = a + b(X)

Excel's regression function can now be used to measure the regression equation and correlation to measure how well the data fits the original projections. So as cash flow data comes in, it is converted to natural log and used to calculate correlation to test how well the results match the projection that was part of the original business plan.

What is needed at this point is to find the antilog which converts natural log back to dollars. The antilog of the natural log (LN) is e^{LN}. In terms of Excel the antilog is =exp(LN).

Month	Cash Flow	log =LN(cash)	antilog =EXP(LN)
1	$1,284	7.16	$1,284
2	$1,649	7.41	$1,649
3	$2,117	7.66	$2,117
4	$2,718	7.91	$2,718
5	$3,490	8.16	$3,490
6	$4,482	8.41	$4,482
7	$5,755	8.66	$5,755
8	$7,389	8.91	$7,389
9	$9,488	9.16	$9,488
10	$12,182	9.41	$12,182
11	$15,643	9.66	$15,643
12	$20,086	9.91	$20,086

Evaluating Actual Cash Flow Results

The above exhibit is the original projected cash flow with the last column being the actual observed cash flow. Based on the original business plan the monthly break-even point was calculated to be $10,000. The actual cash flow shows that during the 12 month period the targeted cash flow goal is met but not as quickly projected.

How Accurate was the original Plan? To answer this question both cash flows need to be converted to natural logs:

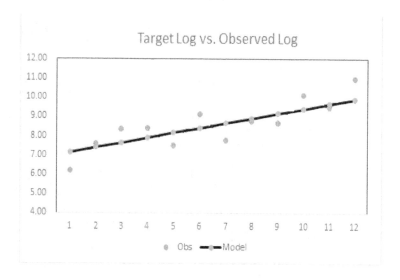

The observed log values do seem to fit the linear function. Excel's regression built-in function can be used to obtain correlation:

SUMMARY OUTPUT

Regression Statistics	
Multiple R	0.84
R Square	0.71
Adjusted R Square	**0.69**
Standard Error	0.70
Observations	12

The R^2 is within a fairly good range for explaining the amount of variance of the observed cash flow by the original assessment. Very few business plans perform exactly as originally laid out. It is always wise to spend time to do a careful examination of original assumptions. If the R2 is 20% then it is imperative to do a thorough review. All the forecasting techniques discussed in this book should be assessed after events start to unfold. It is an education process that will enhance the abilities of all business people to anticipate and handle potential risks. This example started with a standard logarithm growth pattern. The actual growth pattern took longer to accelerate but it was still sufficient for a cash flow turnaround in around a year.

Concluding remarks

There's an old saying in business: "If you can measure it, you can manage it". What's measurable is almost always presented in the form of statistics. Growing a business without the use of statistics is like having one hand tied behind your back in a fight. In small businesses statistical tools and analysis, as discussed in this book, help banks make decisions on whether to offer loans, loans that can be used to grow an existing or starting a new firm. Interpretation of key statistics is essential to decision making. Statistical analysis allows businesses to measure the performance of a business and identify trends. This allows managers to make sound judgments, knowing their decisions are based on data and not on assumptions. Statistics helps businesses to plan better and make predictions about the road ahead.

Appendix I – Random Sampling and IRS Directives

Sample Selection - Excel and IRS Directives

Recently the Internal Revenue Service has promoted the use of and published specific requirements concerning the statistical audit. We have published a summary of the IRS promotion for the use of statistical projections. The premise of this manual is that Excel is a useful aid in carrying out the statistical audit. However, there are two thorny issues regarding the use of Excel. One, it can be very cumbersome when dealing with very large data sets. We have discussed this in our Working Smart series. The second is, does Excel conform to random sample selection standards as published by the Internal Revenue Service?

IRS Specifications for Random Sampling

A random sample using Excel in accordance with IRS Directives has to be carefully designed and explained. The specific wording of the pertinent IRS directive is:

Taxpayers must retain adequate documentation to support the statistical application, sample unit findings, and all aspects of the sample plan and execution. The execution of the sample must be documented and include information for each of the following:

(1) The seed or starting point of the random numbers;

(2) The pairing of random numbers to the frame along with supporting information to retrace the process;

(3) List of the sampling units selected and the results of the evaluation of each unit;

(4) Supporting documentation such as notes, invoices, purchase orders, project descriptions, etc., which support the conclusion reached about each sample item;

(5) The calculation of the projected estimate(s) to the population, including the computation of the standard error of the estimate(s);

(6) A statement as to any slips or blemishes in the execution of the sampling procedure and any pertinent decision rules; and

(7) Computation of all associated adjustments. (An example of an associated adjustment would be the amount of depreciation allowable based on a probability determination of an amount capitalized).

Items 2-7 deal with the linking of random numbers to the book of accounts, proper documentation and estimate methodology. With Auditmetrics CAATS each transaction in the audit population is assigned a "Transaction_ID" and when a sample is selected each transaction in the sample has the Transaction_ID to link back to the audit population.

Pseudorandom Process

A random sample of a book of transactions is a process whereby each transaction has an equal probability of being selected and forms what is referred to as the uniform distribution. A true random process is one in which each selected item does not predict or have influence on the next item to be selected. For example, if you go to a casino and play roulette, each number that comes up is totally independent of those that have preceded it.

However, using a true random process would be a very cumbersome. In the age of computer technology, it is very helpful and time saving if we design a computer algorithm to generate a series of random numbers that follow the uniform distribution. A starting point is to link a series of random numbers to a book of transactions. One standard way is to use an algorithm that starts with a seed number to generate a series of random numbers. For example, in the past we have used the millisecond reading from the computer's clock as a seed to generate a set of random numbers. The selection of the seed number in this instance is also a random process. This method can be more
properly defined as a pseudorandom process.

A pseudorandom sequence of numbers exhibits statistical randomness while being generated by an entirely predictable mathematical process.

Such a convenient methodology has the added benefit that with the same seed number one can produce exactly the same set of numbers. This is of value when sharing results with the IRS or other reviewers. With the same seed number, all parties can replicate the same random sample.

All major statistical software products such as SAS or STATA offer random processes with an option to use a seed number. But some software such as Excel and Auditmetrics do not. Auditmetrics offers a work around. The value of the seed number is for all parties to have the same random number sequence attached to a given set of transactions. Auditmetrics random sampling frame is stratified random sampling which is a very efficient method of sampling. The seed number criteria listed above would make documentation cumbersome by requiring a seed number for each stratum and segmenting the book of transactions to match each stratum Auditmetrics links all sample items to audit population items so that all parties can examine the same set of data, i.e. the flow from the total book to sample.

An example using Excel

Microsoft documentation states that Excel's RAND function is seeded using the "system time" of the computer without much additional elaboration. Using a specific seed number is not possible. To get around this the first step is to link each transaction to a unique identifier. MS Access has a field format "AutoNumber" which numbers each transaction from "1" for the first record and incrementally up to the total number of the transactions. You can also accomplish this in Excel. For example if the first data point in column A1 is set at 1, then the second data point A2 is set A1+1. Then paste cell A2 to the end of the list of transaction in column A. Once that is done copy all of the transactions in the A column and paste special them in the same column as values.

Step 1: Set up Account Transaction ID

As previously discussed crate a transaction ID that uniquely identifies each individual transaction. <u>Be sure it is stored as a value and not in the formula form.</u>

ID	Amount	and. Numt
1	$2.00	=RAND()
2	$27.99	Etc.
3	$5.00	.
Etc.	$39.99	.
.	$39.99	.
.	$27.99	.
.	$5.00	.

Step 2: Generate Random Numbers

Use the formula "=Rand()" to generate a random number in a range between 0 and 1. In this example we want to sample 5 records from a population of 16.

Step 3: Copy Formula to all of the Transactions

ID	Amount	Rand. Numb.
1	$2.00	0.427605523
2	$27.99	0.08021559
3	$5.00	0.633252842
4	$39.99	0.847478392
5	$39.99	0.520001836

Step 4: Copy and Paste Random Numbers

With Excel every time you make changes to the spread sheet it also generates a new set of random numbers. This defeats the purpose of the seed number. By using the **paste / value option** you convert the random sequence to an unchangeable set of values. You now have a column with a single set of random numbers tied to a single transaction. This fulfills the use of a seed number in that you have the ability to generate the same random sample:

ID	Amount	Rand. Numb.
1	$2.00	0.427605523
2	$27.99	0.08021559
3	$5.00	0.633252842
4	$39.99	0.847478392
5	$39.99	0.520001836

Step 5: Select Your Random Sample

Now sort your dataset in ascending order of your random number column.

ID	Amount	Rand. Numb.
15	$24.95	0.034160693
7	$5.00	0.037375766
11	$5.00	0.039393253
8	$27.99	0.164479651
1	$2.00	0.263221827
4	$39.99	0.264010164
9	$5.00	0.29091256
3	$5.00	0.312633768

6	$27.99	0.580692169
12	$1.29	0.62638731
2	$27.99	0.632090533
5	$39.99	0.729794316
14	$1.00	0.820569679
13	$1.29	0.867714912
16	$24.95	0.94713915
10	$24.95	0.953753009

You now have all transactions in a random order. You can take the first 5, last 5 or middle 5 records for a sample of size n=5. Just keep track of your decision rule.

Step 6: Sample n=5

ID	Amount	Rand. Numb.
15	$24.95	0.034160693
7	$5.00	0.037375766
11	$5.00	0.039393253
8	$27.99	0.164479651
1	$2.00	0.263221827

Appendix II – Converting QuickBooks® Standard Reports into Auditmetrics® Data Entry Files

This appendix deals with converting QuickBooks Excel reports into a format that can be readily read in by Auditmetrics as a input data file. The basic process is generic and can be used for any report in Excel from any other Accounting information system.

QuickBooks Excel Data Conversion

The latest version of Auditmetrics relies on standardized data for input and output. The data standard is text files of two types: .txt and .csv files. Auditmetrics data input is the tab delimited text file (.txt). The sample data output is both the tab delimited text file (.txt) and comma separated value file (.csv) which is also a text file. The .csv file has the advantage that it can be readily read in by Excel. It has all the functionality of a spreadsheet and immediately can be saved as a spreadsheet.

Intuit QuickBooks operates in the small business market, sized at approximately 29 million businesses in the United States, and has more than 80% market share with small businesses that use financial management software. QuickBooks uses a "closed" database structure that you cannot access directly. If you want to extract transaction data, such as invoices or checks, you have to use a third party tool to extract data (or get the SDK/ programming toolkit and write your own program). An internet search will reveal several third party vendors to obtain data from QuickBooks.

Data for Auditmetrics has to be in either a .csv or a tab delimited .txt file. These universal file structures make it possible to plugin data from QuickBooks standard reports *without the need for specialized software*. It works best with reports that detail data at the transaction level such as sales, expenses, accounts payable, accounts receivable etc. Reports that detail a summary at a sufficient detail is also useful. For example accounts receivables per customer (price x quantity) is a useful detail. Below is an example using a "Sales by Customer Report" in the Report section of QuickBooks.

Excel data files converted to text files can become seamless plugins to Auditmetrics. However most Excel spreadsheet reports are not specifically formatted as a rectangular data Matrix. A data matrix is a rectangular layout where the top row is the variable name. Each column is the individual variable and each row is the individual record. For example there are standard QuickBooks reports that can be exported to Excel.

In this exercise *QuickBooks Desktop Pro* is used to export a "sales by customer report" from the sample learning database to ultimately create a plugin for Auditmetrics. QuickBooks can generate reports in many different formats.

Below is a report with conversion options. Select **Excel** as the output for the standard report.

Sample Report

	Type	Date	Num	Name	Item	Qty	Amount	Balance
Ecker Design								
	Invoice	12/15/2021	131	Ecker D	Garde	1.00	1.00	1.00
	Invoice	12/15/2021	131	Ecker D	Pest C	1.00	1.00	2.00
Total Ecker Design						2.00	2.00	2.00
Golliday								
75 Sunset Rd.								
	Invoice	12/02/2021	120	Gollida	Plants	10.00	10.00	10.00
	Invoice	12/02/2021	120	Gollida	Install	54.00	54.00	64.00
Total 75 Sunset Rd.						64.00	64.00	64.00
Golliday Sporting G						64.00	64.00	64.00
Heldt, Bob								
	Invoice	12/08/2021	123	Heldt, I	Plants	2.00	2.00	2.00
---------->	Invoice	12/08/2021	123	Heldt, I	Plants	3.00	3.00	5.00
	Invoice	12/08/2021	123	Heldt, I	Fertili	6.00	6.00	11.00

The QuickBooks Report menu bar at the top drop-down list has an option to generate Excel files. One can either generate a new file or add to an existing file. The problem with exporting to a standard report Excel worksheet is it will have the same layout as a printed report hardcopy. An Excel file for the report can be readily converted to a .csv file which is in reality a text file.

Invoice data are embedded and not readily reachable as data elements for processing by Auditmetrics. There is a Report option that will help in selecting invoice data. Once you select the Excel option you are then asked to where to send the report. Select the last option to create a .csv text file. **If you are not using QuickBooks but another accounting system, any Excel report can be converted to .csv by using "save as" and selecting .csv.**

The Report option in this exhibit is not to generate a worksheet but to obtain a .csv file which is a text file readable by Excel. It may look like an ordinary spreadsheet but it is a special text file that can be manipulated and used to create a rectangular text file that can be plugged into Auditmetrics.

Below is the QuickBooks Excel spreadsheet report converted to a .CSV text file:

Type	Date	Num	Name	Amount
Crenshaw, Bob				
Invoice	**12/10/2021**	**FC 8**	**Crenshaw, Bob**	**$60.00**
Total Crenshaw, Bob				
DJ's Computers				
Invoice	**12/15/2021**	**132**	**DJ's Computers**	**$125.00**
Total DJ's Computers				
Ecker Design				
Invoice	**12/15/2021**	**131**	**Ecker Design**	**$23.00**
Invoice	**12/15/2021**	**131**	**Ecker Design**	**$68.00**
Total Ecker Design				

You can use Excel to read in the .csv text file and now it is easy to manipulate. **Sort the .CSV file by Type and Date that are highlighted above.**

Type	Date	Num	Name	Amount
Invoice	12/10/2021	FC 8	Crenshaw, Bob	$60.00
Invoice	12/15/2021	132	DJ's Computers	$125.00
Invoice	12/15/2021	131	Ecker Design	$23.00
Invoice	12/15/2021	131	Ecker Design	$68.00
Crenshaw, Bob				
Total Crenshaw, Bob				
DJ's Computers				
Total DJ's Computers				
Ecker Design				
Total Ecker Design				

All of the invoices are bunched together and now it is a simple matter to remove all extraneous rows and come up with a **rectangular dataset ready for analysis**.

Add Auditmetrics Required Variables:

Amount, Absamt, Transaction_ID and DataSet.

Num	Amount	Absamt	Transaction_ID	DataSet
131	($23.00)	$23.00	3	Run_1
FC 8	$60.00	$60.00	1	Run_1
131	$68.00	$68.00	4	Run_1
132	$125.00	$125.00	2	Run_1

The highlighted columns in gray are required variables for an Auditmetrics text file. Amount was already part of the QuickBooks dataset. But added are three other required variables Absamt,

Transaction_ID, and DataSet. These variable names are required for an Auditmetrics data matrix:

1. **Amount** – The transaction of interest in the analysis.
2. **Absamt** – Absolute value of each transaction. The data set <u>must</u> be sorted in an ascending order. This is to handle credits.
3. **Transaction_ID** – an identifier for each record, it is a record count.
4. **DataSet** – A name to identify this specific dataset.
5. **Primary Key Optional** – If a dataset is from a relational database with a primary key that links the various data tables it is prudent to include this variable in the audit population dataset to be sampled.

Variables 1 to 4 names must be in the data file and spelled exactly as above, letter case and order do not matter. If not present, Auditmetrics will reject the file. The same is true if Absamt is not sorted in ascending order.

If you need to add or create other variables it is safest to use letters and numbers with no embedded spaces. For example if you want to name a variable Run 1 It is best to use Run _1 or Run1. This rule is true for many data base and statistical software.

Transaction_ID has value especially when the data set is the merging of several data sources. For example, if you have two data sets of 1000 each and use MS Access to merge them then Transaction_ID 1 to 1000 are from the first dataset and 1001 to 2000 are from the second dataset.

The worksheet is now ready to be "saved as" a tab delimited .TXT Comma variable separated (.csv) files are standard text files for data transfer but for Auditmetrics only Tab delimited file are required for input because with many .csv files commas may be embedded in many fields such as the "Name" field listed below:

89

Made in the USA
Monee, IL
30 March 2021